Young and Black in AFRICA

Young and Black in AFRICA

compiled with introductory notes by A. Okion Ojigbo

A VINTAGE SUNDIAL BOOK
RANDOM HOUSE · NEW YORK

Acknowledgment is gratefully extended to the following for permission to reprint from their works:

Doubleday & Company, Inc.: From I WILL TRY, by Legson Kayira. Copyright © 1965 by Legson Kayira.

Harcourt Brace Jovanovich, Inc.: From I WAS A SAVAGE, by Prince Modupe. Copyright © 1957 by Harcourt Brace Jovanovich, Inc.

Praeger Publishers, Inc. and Heinemann Educational Books Ltd.: From THE NARROW PATH, by Francis Selormey, 1966.

Praeger Publishers, Inc. and Routledge & Kegan Paul Ltd.: From CHILD OF TWO WORLDS, by R. Mugo Gatheru, 1964.

Alfred A. Knopf, Inc.: From TELL FREEDOM, by Peter Abrahams. Copyright 1954 by Alfred A. Knopf, Inc.

East African Publishing House, Nairobi, Kenya and Charity Wanjiku Waciuma: From DAUGHTER OF MUMBI, 1969.

Acknowledgment is also extended to Dean Babs Fafunwa for permission to reprint his article entitled "An African's Adventures in America," which first appeared in the *Chicago Defender*.

First Vintage Sundial Edition, January 1973. Originally published by Random House, Inc., in 1971.

Library of Congress Cataloging in Publication Data
Ojigbo, A. Okion, comp. Young and Black in Africa.
(A Vintage sundial book, VS-2)   1. Africa—Social life and customs.
I. Title.   [DT14.O38 1973]   916.03'08   72-3120
ISBN 0-394-70802-4

To all the children in the Ojigbo Family,
dead and living, and the many more to come

C O N T E N T S

Young and Black in AFRICA

Foreword

Malcolm X once said that a man without a culture of his own is like a tree without roots. It is a person's culture that sustains him at a time of crisis and adds richness to his life.

For the youth of Africa today, the question of culture is of immediate importance. Young people from the more than fifty different African nations are increasingly coming into contact with the Western world. They are beginning to ask themselves some difficult questions. Which of their proud traditions and rich African customs do they wish to preserve? Which elements of modern Western life do they wish to adopt? What does it mean to be African in today's world?

Until very recently most books about Africa and Africans were written by outsiders. But if a non-African truly wants to understand Africa, he should listen to what Africans have to say about their own way of life.

In this book Africans speak for themselves.

A. OKION OJIGBO

1

Prince Modupe

Prince Modupe

In the following selection Prince Modupe describes his
first trip from his home to the city of Konakry (now
Conakry, the capital of the Republic of Guinea).

Anyone who moves from the country to the city, even in
the United States, is likely to feel strange at first. This
feeling of newness and strangeness is also true for an African
moving to the city. The contrast between country life and
city life is probably even greater in Africa than in America.

I can still remember my first ride in a car. It looked as
if the trees beside the road were moving in one direction
just as fast as the car was moving in the other direction.
But at the same time I was sure those trees were standing
still!

And then my first experience in an airplane. It was a
night flight. When I gathered up my courage to look out
the window, I was amazed. It seemed that the tiny lights
down there must be stars! Was the sky below us? Were we
flying upside down?

Another strange experience was in the subway. To think
that we were actually traveling *through* the ground like an
earthworm, but much faster! How could I ever explain a
subway to an elder in my village who has never left home?

Prince Modupe had an adventurous spirit, which brought

him to the United States in search of education at the age of twenty. He describes his adventures in his autobiography, which he ironically called *I Was a Savage*. The book has been republished as *A Royal African*.

In the book he tells how he killed his first wild animal, a leopard, to prove his manhood at the age of sixteen. He also tells about tracking an elephant, and waiting for it to die, so that he could cut off the tusks and sell them to earn money for his passage to the United States.

As Prince Modupe says, he knew that he had to "get used to strange customs." He indeed learned to do so. He now lives in Los Angeles, where he has been an actor, a movie director, a producer, a professor of anthropology— and has even cut a record disk. Prince Modupe is now raising funds in the United States in preparation for returning to Nigeria to found a badly needed school.

I Meet Money

The villagers stood on the bank of the Scarcis to see me off to the world outside. Kende [my future wife] stood beside my mother in the front ranks. The pain of parting, especially from those two, almost unmanned me. Would they ever see me again? They feared not. In one way, they were right. When I returned several years later, I was not the same person who had left.

Muddy-tan water lapped at the sides of the dugout. Mapam, an older warrior, sat in front; I at the stern.

A few strokes and we were in midstream. Although I was busy with my *batai*, the paddle, I saw through tear-blur their gallant efforts to wave. The dugout swept easily around a bend and we were out of sight.

A trip down the Scarcis is not easy. There are mud flats studded with crocodiles, there is quicksand, and in my day it was the vast playground of the river horses, the hippopotamuses. They are not man-eaters but they love to frolic and when any creature of almost elephant size gets playful with a human, it is dangerous. They love to submerge and surface, cavorting with the zest of a small-boy child. If one comes up under a canoe or even brushes the side of the shell-frail craft, over it goes. The crocodiles seem to be grinning hideously as they wait and watch with small evil eyes.

The first hippo we saw crossed directly in front of us. Others followed into the water, diving and breaking surface. There were too many of them to be traceable. All we could do was to alert ourselves and hope. One of them came up so close to us that my *batai* struck him at the finish of the stroke. Mapam and I ceased paddling; our full concern was to balance the craft by throwing our weights to one side. It steadied, settled. We bent again to our paddles. It was important to go as far as possible by daylight.

There were few places on the bank where it seemed safe to stop. Reeds grew in the shallow water near shore. The banks were lined with huge trees, thick and twisted with lianas, making a screen and a mystery of what lay behind. Brilliant birds perched on overhanging limbs like noisy flowers. Monkeys played on the lianas, chattering defiance at our dugout. Toward evening we spied game at land's edge, antelope, chevrotain. We heard an elephant trumpet in the distance.

For the most part, the day slipped away as quietly as the dugout glided. Yet it seemed more adventurous to me than anything which had happened previously because of the unknown quality of life ahead. Those things which had gone into making me a "complete savage"—the Bondo training, the test of manhood, the judgment poisonings and the sacrificial executions I had witnessed—were the expected shapes and colors of tribal life in the bush. I had been prepared for them since birth. For the unknown ahead I had no qualification except a burning desire to know.

When night fell we lit a palm-oil lamp in the dugout and continued to paddle in the moonless darkness. Crocodiles lie up on mud banks and sand flats at night. If we were lucky enough to avoid going aground on one of those, we would be all right. The hazard of the river was less than the dangers of the unknown, jungle-choked shore. We ate some food we had brought with us and continued down stream.

The morning of the next day we reached the village where it had been arranged on the drums that Paul Boolama [an African Christian] was to wait for me.

6

As I stepped from the dugout, he grasped my hand and wrung it, laughing at the startled expression on my face. Shaking hands was, he explained, the Christian mode of greeting a friend.

I tucked this bit of information away for future use. I believe it would be safe to say that during my early years as a Christian, I was one of the most persistent of all handshakers. I shook the hand of everyone I met, man, woman, or child, often to the surprise or annoyance of the shakee. To thrust forward the hand was my first lesson in the rituals of civilization, learned on the bank of the muddy Scarcis.

After we had rested, Mapam started back toward Dubricka alone, paddling against the current. A great pang clutched my heart as I watched him slowly disappear from view. Paul Boolama and I prepared to go in the other direction. The other direction! The river flows to the sea. Tides push it back upon itself for a space, then the tide reverses, is with the current and all is swept before it. The waters of rivers merge with the sea.

A warrior sat in the front, another in the back of the new dugout. Paul Boolama and I sat between them. This was a larger boat. I asked for a *batai*. Paul explained that we would talk and the others would row. This seemed strange to me because I seemed to be the youngest member of the party, but then I supposed I would have to get used to all sorts of reversals of custom. Boolama was highly pleased that he was able to bring a protégé to his big-father, the missionary with whom he lived. He explained that after we reached Konakry he would send word to Freetown and arrange for my passage in a huge boat. The big-father in Sierra Leone would meet my boat in Freetown. He tried to make me understand that the message would be sent by something called a telegram rather than by talking drums, but I could make nothing of that.

For one thing, I was too appalled at the news that Boolama was not going the entire journey with me. He had to visit more tribes in Guinea and give instruction in places he would revisit before he came back to Freetown. He was a Bambara, and so the logical one to attend to the work in Guinea. I would be perfectly safe on the big coastal boat, he explained.

It was the beginning of a clear night when we approached Konakry. The water was choppy with tide wash and breeze. We swung around a bend. There before my eyes was the dazzling sight of the lights of the coastal city. The grandeur of those lights to my eyes, accustomed to palm-oil lamps, balks any effort of description. Thrill and disbelief quivered through me.

The lights were shut off for a moment by a bend in the river. I thought they had been an illusion. They reappeared and were constantly visible like a skyful of stars snared in a net and brought to earth. Nothing in the missionary's kit of pictures conveyed the lovely sublimity of heaven as did those twinkling lights in front of me.

We passed the blurred outlines of huts of such size as I had never dreamed possible. In the wide span of water before us, huge canoes with smoke coming out of their round tops lay offshore. The dugout was turned toward the docks. These high piles of wooden structure frightened me as did all else. Only Paul Boolama's presence at my side gave me courage to keep my eyes open.

I was wearing my jungle attire. I was nude to the waist and had my spear and knives and bow and arrows. These were sufficient equipment to meet any unknown or known danger in the bush. I clutched them tighter, wondering whether they would be adequate to the dangers of the world. The dugout was steadied for us. Boolama climbed out and I followed.

People on the dock stared at me and pointed. I had my full growth and was well muscled from an active life. I must have looked the savage that I was. The dock loungers could not have known that my heart pommeled my ribs with hard-knocking fear.

Boolama left me for a moment to find a conveyance, telling me to stay where I was and wait for him. Nearby I saw an African woman seated on the ground. Beside her was a calabash filled with *akara*, fried bean bread. I was hungry and it was good to see a familiar kind

9

of food. She held some up to me, speaking in a language I did not understand. I accepted it and began eating.

She spoke out sharply and held up her empty hand with the palm raised. I did not understand. This must be some other ritual of the hands in the outer world. A small crowd gathered quickly as she shrilled at me. I would have run except that Boolama had told me with emphasis to stay where he left me.

A white-uniformed man came over and spoke sharply to me. I could not understand him either. He gestured for my weapons. I was not about to give those up without a struggle. I kept on eating because I was hungry and because I reasoned that if something terrible was about to happen to me, it would only be worse on an empty stomach. The uniformed man put a whistle to his lips and blew on it. The sound was more penetrating than the burr-r-ing of *agoton* [alarm clock]. Two more men came riding up on shiny-wheeled affairs. The crowd thinned at the sweep of their hands.

Paul Boolama came running to me just in time. He said something to the policemen which satisfied them and he drew something shiny out of his pocket which satisfied the African woman.

We went to Boolama's friends in an affair which seemed like a small hut on wheels. On our way he tried to make me understand what money was and its uses. Food was not given for nothing in the civilized world. In fact, almost nothing one wanted could be had without money. It was the most important single thing to have and to know about.

I was baffled. In our village everything we needed for food, clothing, shelter, entertainment, weapons, religion, was furnished by the Great Mother, Earth. If there was some small thing we lacked such as a Foulah pot, we traded something we had to obtain it. I had met money, but I did not understand it. All I understood was an implication of the terrors of needing it and not having it.

Paul Boolama showed me a coin and explained how much rice it would purchase. My father had brought home similar coins from his trips to the coast. They were viewed by the women in our household as suitable source material for bangles to wear at the neck. Our village had no other use for silver.

How was one ever to learn the relative value of these shiny little disks! The only thing we had which was in any way comparable was the cowrie shell, and a big one was not worth more than a slightly smaller one. From this to-do about money, I began to suspect that civilization was complicated. I was shaken by a great fear that I would never be able to master the complications.

At the home of Boolama's friends, clothes were brought for me. He helped me bathe and dress. The thing in which I bathed repulsed me because the used water stayed right there until one had finished, instead of sliding away like the stream water at home. The clothes seemed too many, too heavy, too tight. And the shoes! It took years for me to get accustomed to shoes. What torture! I knew I would have to get used to strange customs but I did not expect any punishment as harsh as having to encase my feet in pinching leather.

Dinner was a nightmare. Was this food, this stuff laid out on a flat dish, a little green here, a little dab of red there, something yellow in one corner? At home everything was cooked together and cooked thoroughly. The meat at this meal was rare. Did Christians eat raw meat like forest beasts? Most frightening of all was the sharp, shiny pronged thing they called a fork. Were these people not at one with each other that they did not eat with their hands from a common bowl?

I tried to do what Boolama did. I stuck my tongue with the fork. The food tasted awful. It needed seasoning, much hot pepper. In the bush it is indication of enmity not to eat proffered food, so I forced it all down, hating every bite, relieved that the portions were what would have seemed meager at home. Perhaps these people ate sparsely because the food was so unpalatable.

Shortly after we arose from the table I had to go into the little room where I had bathed and toileted.

My stomach would not agree to keep the food I had made it accept.

I took off the leather which was torturing my feet and the socks which made them so hot. I sat on the rim of the open toilet bowl thinking about the hardships which seemed to go with being a Christian. Being a savage was certainly more comfortable!

Boolama came looking for me, calling my name. I stood up dizzily and replied. The back of my pants were wet from the water in the bowl. He took one look at me and led me to a cot in the next room. Just as I was, wet pants and all, I fell asleep. I dreamed of converging policemen blowing whistles and swinging clubs because I lacked something called money. Thus passed my first twenty-four hours in civilization.

Olaudah Equiano

Olaudah Equiano

In "Seized Into Slavery" Olaudah Equiano tells how he was kidnapped in Nigeria when he was eleven years old. Being sold from master to master, he moved down the River Niger to the Gulf of Guinea on West Africa's coast. There he was taken aboard a slave ship for the terrible voyage to the New World. The year was 1756.

Slavery existed in Africa, as well as in other parts of the world, before the arrival of Europeans. However, slavery in Africa was very different from what the world later knew it to be. Slaves in Africa, usually prisoners of war, had rights and were generally treated with respect. Their position in the society could be compared to that of indentured servants in the American colonies.

Many of the early settlers in the colonies were indentured servants who had agreed to work without wages for a fixed number of years in return for their transportation to America. The first Africans who came to this country, including those who first arrived in Jamestown in 1619, were treated as such.

Unfortunately the condition of slaves in the New World changed later. Slaves came to be considered not as people but as property. Totally inhuman treatment of them was permitted by law.

If slavery in the New World was so harsh and cruel, why did Africans cooperate with the slave traders? The Europeans ensured their cooperation by bringing guns to Africa. They deceived African rulers, forcing them to wage wars against each other in order to take prisoners as slaves. Africans who refused to accept guns were powerless, and they often became slaves themselves. In self-defense, therefore, Africans were forced into the slave trade. Besides, it had become a good business.

Although millions of Africans died during slave raids or crossing the Atlantic, and many more died in the New World, Equiano fortunately survived. In Virginia he was bought by a plantation owner, who soon sold him to a British naval officer. His new master changed Equiano's name to Gustavus Vassa and took him on naval expeditions to Canada and the Mediterranean.

Equiano wanted to buy his freedom, for which he needed about $200. Beginning with three cents as capital, he started trading on his voyages. By the age of twenty-one he saved enough money—and became a free man.

He continued to sail the seas. He was a member of the Arctic Expedition of 1773, which tried to find a Northwest Passage to the Pacific, hunting walruses and polar bears along the way. He also voyaged to Central America, where he lived for some time with the Mosquito Indians of Honduras.

Equiano continually thought of his homeland. He applied to the Bishop of London to be sent to Africa as a Christian missionary. But his request was denied.

He actively protested against the slave trade and helped to arouse British opinion against it. In 1788 he handed a petition to the Queen of England, asking her to persuade her husband (King George III) to free British slaves in the West Indies.

The next year he published his autobiography, *The Interesting Narrative of the Life of Olaudah Equiano, or Gustavus Vassa the African, Written by Himself*, from which the following selection has been taken. It was a very popular book and was reprinted many times both in Great Britain and in the United States. Thus Olaudah Equiano was one of the earliest and most effective leaders of the abolition movement against slavery.

Equiano married an Englishwoman in 1792. He died in London five years later.

Seized Into Slavery

My father, besides many slaves, had a numerous family, of which seven lived to grow up, including myself and a sister, who was the only daughter. As I was the youngest of the sons, I became the greatest favorite with my mother, and was always with her, and she used to take particular pains to form my mind. I was trained up from my earliest years in the art of war. My daily exercise was shooting and throwing spears, and my mother adorned me with emblems after the manner of our greatest warriors. In this way I grew up till I was turned the age of eleven, when an end was put to my happiness in the following manner.

Generally when the grown people in the neighborhood were gone far in the fields to labor, the children assembled together in some of the neighbors' yards to play. And commonly some of us used to get up a tree to look out for any assailant, or kidnapper, that might come upon us. For they sometimes took those opportunities of our parents' absence to attack and carry off as many as they could seize.

One day, as I was watching at the top of a tree in our yard, I saw one of those people come into the yard of our next neighbor but one, there being many sturdy young people in it. Immediately on this I gave the alarm, and the rogue was surrounded by the sturdiest of them, who tied him with cords so that he could not escape till some of the grown people came and secured him.

But alas! before long it was my fate to be thus attacked and to be carried off when none of the grown people were nigh.

One day, when all our people were gone out to their work as usual, only I and my dear sister were left to mind the house. Two men and a woman got over our walls and in a moment seized us both. Without giving us time to cry out or make resistance, they stopped our mouths and ran off with us into the nearest wood. Here they tied our hands and continued to carry us as far as they could.

When night came on, we reached a small house,

where the robbers halted for refreshment and spent the night. We were then unbound but were unable to take any food. Being quite overpowered by fatigue and grief, our only relief was some sleep, which allayed our misfortune for a short time.

The next morning we left the house and continued traveling all the day. For a long time we had kept to the woods, but at last we came into a road which I believed I knew. I had now some hopes of being rescued. We had advanced but a little way before I observed some people at a distance, at which I began to cry out for their assistance. But my cries had no other effect than to make the kidnappers tie me more tightly and stop my mouth, and then they put me into a large sack. They also stopped my sister's mouth and tied her hands. In this manner we proceeded till we were out of the sight of these people.

When we went to rest the following night they offered us some food. But we refused it and the only comfort we had was in being in one another's arms all that night, and bathing each other with our tears.

But alas! we were soon deprived of even the small comfort of weeping together. The next day proved a day of greater sorrow than I had yet experienced. For my sister and I were then separated, while we lay clasped in each other's arms. It was in vain that we pleaded with them not to part us. She was torn from me and immediately carried away, while I was left in a state of distraction not to be described. I cried and grieved continually, and for several days did not eat anything but what they forced into my mouth.

At length, after many days traveling during which I had often changed masters, I got into the hands of a chieftain in a very pleasant country. This man had two wives and some children, and they all treated me extremely well. They did all they could to comfort me, particularly the first wife, who was something like my mother.

Although I was a great many days journey from my father's house, yet these people spoke exactly the same language with us. This first master of mine, as I may call him, was a smith. My principal employment was working his bellows, which were the same kind as I had seen in my vicinity. They were in some respects not unlike the stove bellows here [in England] in gentlemen's kitchens, and they were covered with leather. In the middle of that leather a stick was fixed. A person stood and worked it, in the same manner as is done to pump water out of a cask with a hand pump. I believe it was gold the smith worked, for it was of a lovely bright yellow color and was worn by the women on their wrists and ankles.

I was there I suppose about a month, and they at last used to trust me some little distance from the house. This liberty I used in embracing every opportunity to inquire the way to my own home. I also sometimes, for the same purpose, went with the maidens in the cool of the evening to bring pitchers of water from the springs for the use of the house. I had also noticed where the sun rose in the morning and set in the evening, as I had traveled along. I had observed that my father's house was toward the rising of the sun.

I therefore determined to seize the first opportunity of making my escape, and to shape my course in that direction. For I was quite oppressed and weighed down by grief for my mother and friends. And my love of liberty, ever great, was strengthened by the mortifying circumstance of not daring to eat with the freeborn children, although I was mostly their companion.

While I was planning my escape, one day an unlucky event happened which put an end to my hopes. I used to be sometimes employed in assisting an elderly woman slave to cook and take care of the poultry. One morning, while I was feeding some chickens, I happened to toss a small pebble at one of them, which hit it in the middle and directly killed it. The old slave, having soon after missed the chicken, inquired after it. On my relating the accident (for I told her the truth, because my mother would never suffer me to tell a lie) she flew into a violent passion and threatened that I should suffer for it. My master being out, she immediately went and told her mistress what I had done. This alarmed me very much and I expected an instant flogging, which to me was uncommonly dreadful, for I had seldom been beaten at home. I therefore resolved to fly, and accordingly I ran into a thicket that was nearby and hid myself in the bushes.

Soon afterward my mistress and the slave returned and, not seeing me, they searched all the house. But not finding me, and I not making answer when they called to me, they thought I had run away, and the whole neighborhood was raised in the pursuit of me.

In that part of the country (as well as ours) the houses and villages were skirted with woods, or shrubberies. The bushes were so thick that a man could readily conceal himself in them so as to elude the strictest search. The neighbors continued the whole day looking for me, and several times many of them came within a few yards of the place where I lay hid. I expected every moment, when I heard a rustling among the trees, to be found out and punished by my master. But they never discovered me, though they were often so near that I even heard their conversation as they were looking about for me.

I learned from them that any attempt to return home would be hopeless. Most of them supposed I had fled toward home. But the distance was so great and the way so intricate that they thought I could never reach it, and that I should be lost in the woods. When I heard this I was seized with a violent panic, and abandoned myself to despair.

Night too began to approach and aggravated all my fears. I had before entertained hopes of getting home and had determined when it should be dark to make the attempt. But I was now convinced it was fruitless. I began to think that, if possibly I could escape all other animals, I could not those of the human kind and that, not knowing the way, I must perish in the woods.

I heard frequent rustlings among the leaves, and being pretty sure they were snakes, I expected every instant to be stung by them. This increased my anguish, and the horror of my situation became now quite insupportable. I at length quitted the thicket, very faint and hungry, for I had not eaten or drunk anything all the day. I crept to my master's kitchen, which was an open shed, and laid myself down in the ashes with an anxious wish for death to relieve me from all my pains.

I was scarcely awake in the morning when the old woman slave, who was the first up, came to light the fire and saw me in the fireplace. She was very much surprised to see me and could scarcely believe her own eyes. She now promised to intercede for me. She went for her master, who soon after came and, having slightly reprimanded me, ordered me to be taken care of and not ill treated.

Soon after this my master's only daughter sickened and died, which affected him so much that for some time he was almost frantic and really would have killed himself had he not been watched and prevented. However, a small time afterward he recovered, and I was again sold.

I was now carried to the left of the sun's rising through many dreary wastes and dismal woods, amidst the hideous roarings of wild beasts. The people I was sold to used to carry me very often when I was tired either on their shoulders or on their backs. I saw many convenient well-built sheds along the road, at proper distances, to accommodate the merchants and travelers, who lay in those buildings along with their wives, who often accompany them. They always go well armed.

From the time I left my own nation I always found somebody that understood me till I came to the seacoast. The languages of different nations did not totally differ. They were therefore easily learned. While I was journeying thus through Africa, I acquired two or three different tongues.

I had been traveling for a considerable time when one evening, to my great surprise, whom should I see brought to the house where I was but my dear sister? As soon as she saw me she gave a loud shriek and ran into my arms. I was quite overpowered. Neither of us could speak. But, for a considerable time, we clung to each other in mutual embraces, unable to do anything but weep. Our meeting affected all who saw us. And indeed I must acknowledge, in honor of those African destroyers of human rights, that I never met with any ill treatment or saw any offered to their slaves, except tying them when necessary to keep them from running away.

When these people knew we were brother and sister they indulged us to be together. The man to whom I supposed we belonged lay with us, he in the middle, while she and I held one another by the hands across his breast all night. And thus for a while we forgot our misfortunes in the joy of being together.

But even this small comfort was soon to have an end. For scarcely had the fatal morning appeared when she was again torn from me forever! I was now more miserable, if possible, than before. The small relief which her presence gave me from pain was gone. The wretchedness of my situation was redoubled by my anxiety after her fate, and my apprehensions lest her sufferings should be greater than mine when I could not be with her to alleviate them.

Yes, thou dear partner of all my childish sports! thou sharer of my joys and sorrows! To that Heaven which protects the weak from the strong, I commit the care of your innocence and virtues, if your youth and delicacy have not long since fallen victims to the violence of the African trader, the pestilential stench of a Guinea ship, or the lash and lust of a brutal and unrelenting overseer.

I did not long remain after my sister. I was again sold and carried through a number of places till, after traveling a considerable time, I came to a town called Tinmah, in the most beautiful country I had yet seen in Africa. It was extremely rich. There were many streams which flowed through it and supplied a large pond in the center of the town, where the people washed.

Here I first saw and tasted coconuts, which I thought superior to any nuts I had ever tasted before. And the trees were also interspersed amongst the houses, which had commodious shades adjoining and were in the same manner as ours, the insides being neatly plastered and whitewashed.

Here I also saw and tasted for the first time sugar cane. Their money consisted of little white shells, the size of the fingernail. I was sold here for 172 of these shells by a merchant who lived and brought me there. I had been about two or three days at his house when a wealthy widow, a neighbor of his, came there one evening, bringing with her an only son, a young gentleman about my own age and size. Here they saw me and, having taken a fancy to me, I was bought from the merchant and went home with them.

Her house and premises were situated close to one of those streams I have mentioned, and were the finest I ever saw in Africa. They were very extensive, and she had a number of slaves to attend her. The next day I was washed and perfumed. When mealtime came, I was led into the presence of my mistress and ate and drank before her with her son.

This filled me with astonishment. I could scarce help expressing my surprise that the young gentleman should allow me, who was a slave, to eat with him who was free. Also, he would not at any time either eat or drink till I had taken first because I was the eldest, which was similar to our own custom. Indeed everything here, and all their treatment of me, made me forget that I was a slave.

The language of these people resembled ours so nearly that we understood each other perfectly. They had also the very same customs as we. There were likewise slaves daily to attend us. My young master and I, with other boys, sported with our darts and bows and arrows as I had been used to do at home. In this resemblance to my former happy state, I passed about two months.

I now began to think I was to be adopted into the family, and was beginning to be reconciled to my situation and to forget by degrees my misfortunes, when all at once the delusion vanished. Without the least previous knowledge, one morning, early, while my dear master and companion was still asleep, I was awakened out of my reverie to fresh sorrow and hurried away.

Thus, at the very moment I dreamed of the greatest happiness, I found myself most miserable. It seemed as if fortune wished to give me this taste of joy, only to render the reverse more poignant. The change I now

experienced was as painful as it was sudden and un-
expected. It was a change indeed from a state of bliss
to a scene which is inexpressible by me. I discovered
an element I had never before beheld, and till then
had no idea of, wherein such instances of hardship and
cruelty continually occurred as I can never reflect on
but with horror.

All the nations and people I had hitherto passed
through resembled our own in their manners, customs,
and language. But I came at length to a country, the
inhabitants of which differed from us in all those par-
ticulars. I was very much struck with this difference,
especially when I came among a people who did not
circumcise, and ate without washing their hands. They
cooked also in iron pots, and had European cutlasses
and crossbows, which were unknown to us, and fought
with their fists among themselves. Their women were
not so modest as ours, for they ate and drank and slept
with their men. But above all, I was amazed to see
no sacrifices or offerings among them.

In some of those places the people ornamented
themselves with scars, and likewise filed their teeth
very sharp. They wanted sometimes to ornament me
in the same manner. But I would not allow them,
hoping that I might sometime be among a people who
did not thus disfigure themselves, as I thought they did.

At last I came to the banks of a large river, which
was covered with canoes, in which the people appeared

to live with their household utensils and provisions of all kinds. I was beyond measure astonished at this, as I had never before seen any water larger than a pond or a stream. And my surprise was mingled with no small fear when I was put into one of these canoes, and we began to paddle and move along the river.

We continued going on thus till night, when we came to land and made fires on the banks, each family by themselves. Some dragged their canoes on shore, others stayed and cooked in theirs and lay in them all night. Those on the land had mats of which they made tents, some in the shape of little houses. In these we slept.

After the morning meal we embarked again and proceeded as before. I was often very much astonished to see some of the women, as well as the men, jump into the water, dive to the bottom, come up again, and swim about.

Thus I continued to travel, sometimes by land, sometimes by water, through different countries and various nations. Finally, at the end of six or seven months after I had been kidnapped, I arrived at the seacoast.

The first object which saluted my eyes when I arrived on the coast was the sea, and a slave ship which was then riding at anchor and waiting for its cargo. These filled me with astonishment, which was soon converted into terror when I was carried on board.

I was immediately handled and tossed up to see if I were sound by some of the crew, and I was now persuaded that I had gotten into a world of bad spirits and that they were going to kill me. Their complexions too differing so much from ours, their long hair and the language they spoke (which was very different from any I had ever heard) united to confirm me in this belief.

I now saw myself deprived of all chance of returning to my native country or even the least glimpse of hope of gaining the shore, which I now considered as friendly. And I even wished for my former slavery in preference to my present situation, which was filled with horrors of every kind, still heightened by my ignorance of what I was to undergo.

Francis Selormey

In Africa the birth of a child is a cause for joy, deserving prayers and sacrifices. Francis Selormey describes the birth of his sister in the following selection from his autobiography, *The Narrow Path*.

Francis was five years old when his sister was born. As an only child he had been quite mischievous. He even operated a "fish racket" to trade away the family's fish for some candies he wanted. When his father discovered his "racketeering," Francis's grandmother saved him from the walloping his father was planning to give him.

His grandmother also helped to deliver Francis's baby sister. In societies where there are no modern doctors or hospitals, older women are skillful midwives. Childbirth is a concern of the whole family, not only parents but grand-

Francis Selormey

parents and Ancestors as well. So Francis's grandmother prayed to the family Ancestors for the safe delivery of the baby.

Like many African Christians, Francis's family also continued to follow African religious traditions. Christian missionaries, who disliked the importance Africans attached to their own traditions, often tried to get rid of African religious ceremonies. But a large number of Christians in Africa still keep an Ancestor shrine in their house or compound—and not just for decoration.

Francis Selormey was born at Dzelukofe, near Keta, in the eastern coastal area of Ghana. After studying physical education both in Ghana and in Germany, he returned home to teach the same subject at a Teachers' Training College in Hohoe, where he started to write seriously. He later moved to the city of Cape Coast to become the Regional Director of the Ghana Sports Council. He now lives in Ghana's capital, Accra, where he is the Director of the Central Organization of Sports.

My Sister Is Born

One evening, as we sat at supper, my mother said, "I am not feeling very well."

"What is the matter?" my father asked.

"Oh," she sighed, "I have been feeling bad all day."

"Yes," agreed my father. "I can see that. Our supper tonight proves it. It has no taste in it. I only ate it to save a quarrel," he added virtuously!

My mother was not to be roused. "You are right,

Efo," she said. Efo is a term of respect meaning literally "brother," and it was the way in which my mother addressed my father at that time. "I could not cook this evening," she continued, "so I told Anny to do it. I have spent most of the day in bed. My back aches so much."

My father became more sympathetic. He called for hot water and a towel with which he applied warmth and massage to my mother's aching back and swollen stomach. He persuaded her to take some pap—a kind of thin gruel made from roasted corn—and finally settled her to rest on her bed. I lay down beside her, my father retired to his own room and soon we were all asleep.

Not for long, however. My mother's cry of pain awoke me and brought my father rushing in from his room. "What is it?" he cried, and my mother told him that the pains were terrible.

My father hurried off to call my grandmother, and I was left alone with my mother. The other members of our household, my mother's maidservants and her young sister, and my father's young brother, were in another part of the compound and had not awoken. I felt unreal—not exactly afraid, but strange and bewildered. I did not know why my mother was in pain.

I went and stood beside her bed and saw her writhing and biting her lips. I remembered that my father had made a towel warm in hot water and held it to her body. I asked her if I should do the same. She looked at me long and lovingly.

"Thank you, my dear son," she said. "But there is nothing you can do. Go to bed."

I was hurt by her answer and went out into the compound. The moon was shining brightly. I felt the spirits around me.

I remembered the words that I had heard from a missionary priest at a First Communion Mass. He had said, "God hears the prayers of little children and loves to answer them. So the children should always remember to pray for their parents."

As I was thinking of this, my eyes fell on the bucket of water and the towel that my father had used earlier in the evening. I clasped my hands and prayed. "Please God, as soon as I put this warm towel on my mother make her stop crying, and get up and feel quite well." Absolutely certain that God would agree to my request, I walked firmly to the bucket of water and picked up the towel and plunged it in. The water was very cold. My heart fell, my faith in the missionary priests and their God was shaken.

I dropped the towel into the cold water and went back to my mother's room. My mother was writhing in agony and did not notice me as I crept into a corner of her room.

Soon my father came back with my grandmother. She began to take the cloths off my mother. My father

35

noticed me and ordered me to go into his room and
lie down on his bed. I went into his room but I hid
myself behind the door and watched through the crack.
I realized now that the baby, which I knew my mother
carried within her body, was about to come out and
I was curious to see how. But then I heard my grandmother telling my father to go quickly and fetch two
other women who were experienced midwives, and I
was afraid he might first come into his room, and so
I went and lay down on my father's bed.

But I was wide awake. My whole body was trembling with curiosity and excitement and fear; my eyes
were unnaturally bright, my ears unnaturally sharp. I
heard my father run through the sitting room, and out
through the main door of the house, into the compound. I heard the gate of the compound unbolted and
slammed again. From my mother's room came my
grandmother's voice murmuring words of encouragement and consolation.

"Do not worry, Edzi. Everything is as it should be.
It will soon be over. Soon you will have another beautiful child." Her gentle voice droned on and on till it
almost lulled me to sleep.

Then the great gate rattled and slammed again, and
my father hurried back with two old women and they
all went into my mother's bedroom. There was a short
consultation in low voices; my mother began to cry
again and then I heard footsteps hurry out into the

compound. I knelt on my father's bed and looked out of the window.

There, in the middle of the compound, I could see a small hut and before it my father, my grandmother and one of the other women standing. Under this hut, I knew, were buried the tools of a powerful ancestor of mine, who had been a blacksmith. We were taught that his spirit lived permanently in this hut and from there he guided and protected his descendants. We called him "Torgbui Zu," which means "Grandfather Anvil."

His house is still there and his spirit is still revered and consulted, petitioned and thanked. But now, his children have replaced his mud hut with a modern house of concrete blocks. Members of the family go to ask for good luck on all they have to do, and after a particular success, or in times of special needs, they put money and other gifts in the little house. I often saw my uncles throw in coins before they went off to fish, and when the catch was good, they made a present of the best fish in the net to Torgbui Zu.

The bolder ones among the children sometimes crept into the little house, collected the money and bought sweets with it. We were told that children who picked up the spirit's good money would undoubtedly grow up to be thieves. Indeed, we had a cousin, Bensah—the third son—was his name, who regularly stole the spirit's presents and did grow up to be a thief. We firmly believed that the spirit had cursed him.

Now, on the night my sister was born, I saw my grandmother, my father and another woman standing before Torgbui Zu's house, and I knelt motionless on my father's bed watching and listening. My father bared his shoulders as a mark of respect and fastened his cloth round his waist. He held in his hand a calabash containing a mixture of corn flour and water. He passed it to my grandmother who, in turn, passed it to the other woman. The woman stepped forward and stirred the calabash with her hand. Then, holding it with her two hands, she raised it to the east and to the west and began to pray aloud.

"Torgbui Zu, and all the family gods, behold us here before dawn this day, at the door of your house. Wake up and come to our aid! We are all as children groping in the darkness of this world. We are powerless and we need your help. The wife of your son, Nani, is laboring to deliver his child. We beg you therefore to go to the first home of the child, and to push it into this world. When we return to the house, let the child be quickly and easily born. You are the only one on whom we can rely. Prove now to us that your spirit does indeed live among us, and works for the welfare of those you have left behind. If you do not assist at the birth of your grandchildren, who will there be to feed you and remember you? Without your help at such times, your family would die out and be lost from

38

the face of the earth. Torgbui Zu, you know more than we. Send this child quickly and easily."

The prayer ended and the solution of corn flour was poured out upon the ground. My grandmother looked carefully at the shape and the pattern that the white mixture made upon the earth, and she interpreted it to mean that Torgbui Zu had heard and accepted the prayer and would see that the child was safely and easily born.

The party went back into my mother's room and told her and her attendant that all was well, and she and the child would be safe.

For some time all was quiet and I silently praised my great ancestor who had taken away my mother's pain, when the God of the missionary priests had failed to help me. Then suddenly, she cried out again and I heard the women exhorting her, "That is right! Do not stop! It is almost here! Now, again!"

I could not stay in bed. I crept out of the bedroom, along the veranda, and into the sitting room. A few minutes later, my father entered the room. He looked at me, but he said nothing. Perhaps he did not see me. He sat silently in one of the armchairs.

The next moment, the cry of a baby ran through the house. My father leaped out of his chair and ran into my mother's bedroom. I began to follow him but he saw me and ordered me to return to his room. From there, I heard my mother ask, "What is it?"

39

And my grandmother replied, "A girl. A beautiful girl."

"It is a big child," one of the women remarked.

"And its lips are beautifully black," the other added.

I crept to the doorway and was in time to see the cord cut with a piece of broken bottle. My father left the house, awoke a nearby storekeeper, and brought back to my mother a bottle of beer which he and the women insisted on her drinking. Then her attendants helped her walk to the bathroom, where they washed and dressed her.

Meanwhile, I watched my grandmother wrap the baby in a cloth and lay her on a new mat on the floor. I crept into the room. My father looked up and smiled at me.

"There is your sister," he said. Without a word, I lay down beside her.

"Be careful, Kofi," my father warned. "Do not disturb your little sister."

I was filled with love for her. I wanted to hold her in my arms, I wanted to shield her from every harm, I wanted to touch her tiny hands. But I lay quiet and still beside her until my mother and her attendants returned in a slow procession. My mother sank back onto her bed which my grandmother had made clean for her. One of the other women picked up the baby and rubbed her all over with palm oil, and wrapped her in a clean cloth and put her into my mother's arms.

This was my sister Ami. Her name was decided for her by the day on which she was born. Her name was Ami because she was born on a Saturday, just as my name is Kofi because I was born on a Friday.

The women went away. My grandmother prepared some breakfast for us all and then returned to her own house. My mother and the baby slept and my father led me away.

Every morning and evening, my grandmother came to attend to my mother and to bathe the baby. She would lift the child from the bed by her two hands and ask, "Are you well, little one?"

My mother would answer, "She says she is feeling fine."

Everyone was very happy.

When my grandmother took the baby, I would climb on to my old place on my mother's bed, and from there I watched my sister being bathed.

My grandmother called for warm water in a bucket, an enamel bowl, and the baby's toilet articles. She would then seat herself on a low stool, stretch her legs out over the enamel bowl, and roll her cloth up to her thighs and tuck it between her legs. A maidservant would arrange a bucket of hot water at the grandmother's right hand, a bowl of cold water on her left, and hand her the baby.

First, the old lady would bathe the baby's head with hot water. Then she would direct that the cold water should be added to the hot until it was lukewarm. Next, with soapy hands, she would wash the baby all over, and rinse her well. The water which she splashed over the baby fell from the grandmother's thighs into the bowl beneath. The baby was not actually put into the water but she was thoroughly washed.

Still sitting in the same position, my grandmother would dry and powder the baby and rub shea butter on to her joints to make them supple. When the baby was a few weeks old, my grandmother used a sponge made from beaten wood pulp instead of her hands, and after the bath would splash cold water on the baby. This worried me because it made the baby cry out as if she were hurt.

The water which collected in the enamel bowl under my grandmother's legs was used to bathe me with. My grandmother insisted on this, because she said it would prevent me from being jealous of the baby.

I had good reason to be jealous of Ami. She took my place on my mother's bed and it seemed to me that my mother gave her all her attention. I now slept beside my father on his bed.

At first I did not like this but soon I became used to it, and then pleased and proud to be there. With Ami's birth, it seemed to me that my father loved me. He beat me less often and less hard, and often he made me happy with kind remarks and little presents. Perhaps the new responsibility I felt as an elder brother made me behave better or perhaps now that my mother had a daughter, my father felt more that I was his son.

When he saw me sitting with my mother, and the baby, he would ask, "Do you want to sit among women?" His voice made me feel that it was not right of me to want to be there, and when he said, "Come and let us go for a walk," I would get up at once and go with him.

The baby brought many visitors to our house. Most of them came with small presents—pieces of cloth, soap, baby's clothes, money or firewood. Those who had nothing to bring filled their buckets with water and carried it to the house. This was a most welcome present in a land where water was sometimes scarce and always had to be carried home.

On the eighth day after her birth, the baby, like every baby of her tribe, was "outdoored." At five o'clock in the morning, just before dawn on that day, my grandparents, my uncles and other relatives assembled before our ancestor's hut. Libation was poured by my grandfather and prayers were offered for his continued protection of the child and her family. The corn-flour solution was poured on the ground to feed the friendly spirits. Then a glass full of locally and illegally brewed gin—a strong drink called "Akpeteshi"—was poured out, that the unfriendly spirits might drink it and become drunk and so forget any evil designs they might have had on the child.

The child was then brought out and laid on the bare ground under the eaves of the blacksmith's hut. A bucket of water was poured onto the thatch so that it dripped down onto the baby and made her scream. This was to symbolize the hardships of the world and to emphasize the need the child has for the care and protection of its family.

One of the women in the group—also an Ami, a Saturday-born—rushed forward and picked up the baby saying, "Whose precious child is this? I have found it. Who will pay me for this child?"

My mother then stepped out of her room for the first time and said, "I will." She paid a token price of a penny and received her child back.

The old women of the party accompanied her back into her room and instructed and advised her on the care of the baby and of her own health. She was told that she could then go out into the open air, but she must wear sandals on her feet, and a kerchief round her head or she would be attacked by the after-birth sickness. She was forbidden to keep the baby out after six o'clock in the evening but she was advised to bring her out into the fresh air at dawn. It was said that the morning dew would make the child grow.

Meanwhile, the other members of the family and the guests assembled in the sitting room, drinks were served and presents of money were given.

In the afternoon, Ami was baptized in the Catholic Church and given a Christian name. My father was happy that evening when all the ceremonies were accomplished. He called me to him and gave me a glass of beer.

"Drink, Kofi," he said. "This is children's day. I have a son and a daughter." I drank the bitter drink eagerly to please my father, and soon I fell asleep.

The party continued. My mother's mother arrived from Lomé, bringing with her many expensive presents. But Ami and I were fast asleep.

Peter Abrahams

Peter Abrahams

In his autobiography, *Tell Freedom*, Peter Abrahams describes what life is like for a black youth in South Africa.

If you are a black person in South Africa today, you cannot vote. You cannot express your opinion, even by peaceful demonstrations. The racist government controls your movements within your own native land.

Although black Africans outnumber whites more than three to one, the government allows them to have only 10 percent of the land. There the Africans must live in extremely poor and overcrowded "reserves" (like the American Indian reservations in the United States). The government keeps black Africans—as well as white people who openly sympathize with them—in prison for months or even years without trial.

Millions of black Africans still live under white racist regimes. In addition to South Africa, these include Zimbabwe (Rhodesia) and the Portuguese colonies of Angola, Mozambique, and Guinea (Bissau). The plight of Africans in such places is a tragic one. After centuries of so-called Portuguese colonial rule in Mozambique only 2 per cent of the Africans there can read and write.

Africans have hoped for world support, particularly

47

through the United Nations. Very unfortunately, resolutions passed by the UN, upholding the fundamental human rights of all Africans, have had little or no effect. Nations that can and should effect changes are unwilling to do so.

The UN has been unable to guarantee the fundamental rights of all Africans because of the veto power held by a few nations in the Security Council. Such nations have repeatedly prevented the UN from driving out the racist governments by force. Such UN member nations also have been unwilling to cut business and diplomatic ties with those oppressive governments.

Peter Abrahams was born in 1919 in the Transvaal, South Africa, of a "colored" mother and an Ethiopian father. ("Colored" is the South African term for a person with white and black ancestry.) Peter spent his early years in the ghetto of Johannesburg. But when his father died he went to live with his Aunt Lisa and Uncle Sam in Elsburg. There in Elsburg, and later back in the slums of Johannesburg, Abrahams experienced the cruelty of racism in South Africa.

Peter Abrahams, one of the world's outstanding authors, fled racist South Africa. He lived for some years in London; he now lives with his wife and three children in Jamaica. In addition to his autobiography his books include *Mine Boy, Path of Thunder, A Wreath for Udomo, A Night of Their Own,* and *This Island, Now.*

Tell Freedom

Wednesday was crackling day. On that day the children of the location made the long trek

to Elsburg siding for the squares of pig's rind that
passed for our daily meat. We collected a double lot
of cow dung the day before; a double lot of *moeroga*
[wild spinach].

I finished my breakfast and washed up. Aunt Liza
was at her washtub in the yard. A misty, sickly sun
was just showing. And on the open veld the frost lay
thick and white on the grass.

"Ready?" Aunt Liza called.

I went out to her. She shook the soapsuds off her
swollen hands and wiped them on her apron. She lifted
the apron and put her hand through the slits of the
many thin cotton dresses she wore. The dress nearest
the skin was the one with the pocket. From this she
pulled a sixpenny piece. She tied it in a knot in the
corner of a bit of coloured cloth and handed it to me.

"Take care of that. . . . Take the smaller piece of
bread in the bin, but don't eat it till you start back.
You can have a small piece of crackling with it. Only
a small piece, understand?"

"Yes, Aunt Liza."

"All right."

I got the bread and tucked it into the little canvas
bag in which I would carry the crackling.

" 'Bye, Aunt Liza." I trotted off, one hand in my
pocket, feeling the cloth where the money was. I
paused at Andries's home.

"Andries!" I danced up and down while I waited.

The cold was not so terrible on bare feet if one did not keep still.

Andries came trotting out of his yard. His mother's voice followed; desperate and plaintive:

"I'll skin you if you lose the money!"

"Women!" Andries said bitterly.

I glimpsed the dark, skinny woman at her washtub as we trotted across the veld. Behind and in front of us, other children trotted in twos and threes.

There was a sharp bite to the morning air I sucked in; it stung my nose so that tears came to my eyes; it went down my throat like an icy draught; my nose ran. I tried breathing through my mouth, but this was worse. The cold went through my shirt and shorts; my skin went pimply and chilled; my fingers went numb and began to ache; my feet felt like frozen lumps that did not belong to me, yet jarred and hurt each time I put them down. I began to feel sick and desperate.

"Jesus God in heaven!" Andries cried suddenly.

I looked at him. His eyes were rimmed in red. Tears ran down his cheeks. His face was drawn and purple, a sick look on it.

"Faster," I said.

"Think it'll help?"

I nodded. We went faster. We passed two children, sobbing and moaning as they ran. We were all in the same desperate situation. We were creatures haunted and hounded by the cold. It was a cruel enemy who gave no quarter. And our means of fighting it were pitifully inadequate. In all the mornings and evenings of the winter months, young and old, big and small, were helpless victims of the bitter cold. Only towards noon and in the early afternoon, when the sun sat high in the sky, was there a brief respite.

For us children, the cold, especially the morning cold, assumed an awful and malevolent personality. We talked of "it." "It" was a half-human monster with evil thoughts, evil intentions, bent on destroying us. "It" was happiest when we were most miserable. Andries had told me how "it" had, last winter, caught and killed a boy.

Hunger was an enemy too, but one with whom we could come to terms, who had many virtues and values. Hunger gave our pap, *moeroga,* and crackling a feast-like quality. When it was not with us, we could think and talk kindly about it. Its memory could even give moments of laughter. But the cold of winter was with us all the time. "It" never really eased up. There were only more bearable degrees of "it" at high noon and on mild days. "It" was the real enemy. And on this Wednesday morning, as we ran across the veld, winter was more bitterly, bitingly, freezingly real than ever.

The sun climbed. The frozen earth thawed, leaving the short grass looking wet and weary. Painfully our feet and legs came alive. The aching numbness slowly left our fingers. We ran more slowly in the more bearable cold.

In climbing, the sun lost some of its damp look and

seemed a real, if cold, sun. When it was right overhead, we struck the sandy road, which meant we were nearing the siding. None of the others were in sight. Andries and I were alone on the sandy road on the open veld. We slowed down to a brisk walk. We were sufficiently thawed to want to talk.

"How far?" I said.

"A few minutes," he said.

"I've got a piece of bread," I said.

"Me too," he said. "Let's eat it now."

"On the way back," I said. "With a bit of crackling."

"Good idea. . . . Race to the fork."

"All right."

"Go!" he said.

We shot off together, legs working like pistons. He soon pulled away from me. He reached the fork in the road some fifty yards ahead.

"I win!" he shouted gleefully, though his teeth still chattered.

We pitched stones down the road, each trying to pitch farther than the other. I won and wanted to go on doing it. But Andries soon grew weary with pitching. We raced again. Again he won. He wanted another race, but I refused. I wanted pitching, but he refused. So, sulking with each other, we reached the pig farm.

We followed a fenced-off pathway round sprawling white buildings. Everywhere about us was the grunt of pigs. As we passed an open doorway, a huge dog came bounding out, snarling and barking at us. In our terror we forgot it was fenced in, and we streaked away. Surprised, I found myself a good distance ahead of Andries. We looked back and saw a young white woman call the dog to heel.

"Damn Boer dog," Andries said.

"Matter with it?" I asked.

"They teach them to go for us. Never get caught by one. My old man's got a hole in his bottom where a Boer dog got him."

I remembered I had outstripped him.

"I won!" I said.

"Only because you were frightened," he said.

"I still won."

"Scare arse," he jeered.

"Scare arse, yourself!"

"I'll knock you!"

"I'll knock you back!"

A couple of white men came down the path and ended our possible fight. We hurried past them to the distant shed where a queue had already formed. There were grown-ups and children. All the grown-ups and some of the children were from places other than our location.

The line moved slowly. The young white man who served us did it in leisurely fashion, with long pauses for a smoke. Occasionally he turned his back.

At last, after what seemed hours, my turn came. Andries was behind me. I took the sixpenny piece from the square of cloth and offered it to the man.

"Well?" he said.

"Sixpence crackling, please."

Andries nudged me in the back. The man's stare suddenly became cold and hard. Andries whispered into my ear.

"Well?" the man repeated coldly.

"Please, *baas,*" I said.

"What d'you want?"

"Sixpence crackling, please."

"What?"

Andries dug me in the ribs.

"Sixpence crackling, please, *baas.*"

"What?"

"Sixpence crackling, please, *baas.*"

"You new here?"

"Yes, *baas.*" I looked at his feet, while he stared at me.

At last he took the sixpenny piece from me. I held my bag open while he filled it with crackling from a huge pile on a large canvas sheet on the ground. Turning away, I stole a fleeting glance at his face. His eyes met mine, and there was amused, challenging mockery in them. I waited for Andries at the back of the queue, out of the reach of the white man's mocking eyes.

The cold day was at its mildest as we walked home along the sandy road. I took out my piece of bread and, with a small piece of greasy crackling, still warm, on it, I munched as we went along. We had not yet made our peace, so Andries munched his bread and crackling on the other side of the road.

"Dumb fool!" he mocked at me for not knowing how to address the white man.

"Scare arse!" I shouted back.

Thus, hurling curses at each other, we reached the fork. Andries saw them first and moved over to my side of the road.

"White boys," he said.

There were three of them, two of about our own size and one slightly bigger. They had school bags and were coming towards us up the road from the siding.

"Better run for it," Andries said.

"Why?"

"No, that'll draw them. Let's just walk along, but quickly."

"Why?" I repeated.

"Shut up," he said.

Some of his anxiety touched me. Our own scrap was forgotten. We marched side by side as fast as we could. The white boys saw us and hurried up the road. We passed the fork. Perhaps they would take the turning away from us. We dared not look back.

55

"Hear them?" Andries asked.

"No." I looked over my shoulder. "They're coming," I said.

"Walk faster," Andries said. "If they come closer, run."

"Hey, *klipkop!*"

"Don't look back," Andries said.

"Hottentot!"

We walked as fast as we could.

"Bloody Kaffir!"

Ahead was a bend in the road. Behind the bend were bushes. Once there, we could run without them knowing it till it was too late.

"Faster," Andries said.

They began pelting us with stones.

"Run when we get to the bushes," Andries said.

The bend and the bushes were near. We would soon be there.

A clear young voice carried to us: "Your fathers are dirty black bastards of baboons!"

"Run!" Andries called.

A violent, unreasoning anger suddenly possessed me. I stopped and turned.

"You're a liar!" I screamed it.

The foremost boy pointed at me. "An ugly black baboon!"

In a fog of rage I went towards him.

"Liar!" I shouted. "My father was better than your father!"

I neared them. The bigger boy stepped between me and the one I was after.

"My father was better than your father! Liar!"

The big boy struck me a mighty clout on the side of the face. I staggered, righted myself, and leaped at the boy who had insulted my father. I struck him on the face, hard. A heavy blow on the back of my head nearly stunned me. I grabbed at the boy in front of me. We went down together.

"Liar!" I said through clenched teeth, hitting him with all my might.

Blows rained on me—on my head, my neck, the side of my face, my mouth—but my enemy was under me and I pounded him fiercely, all the time repeating:

"Liar! Liar! Liar!"

Suddenly stars exploded in my head. Then there was darkness.

I emerged from the darkness to find Andries kneeling beside me.

"God, man! I thought they'd killed you."

I sat up. The white boys were nowhere to be seen. Like Andries, they'd probably thought me dead and run off in panic. The inside of my mouth felt sore and swollen. My nose was tender to the touch. The back of my head ached. A trickle of blood dripped from my

57

nose. I stemmed it with the square of coloured cloth. The greatest damage was to my shirt. It was ripped, in many places.

I remembered the crackling. I looked anxiously about. It was safe, a little off the road on the grass. I relaxed. I got up and brushed my clothes. I picked up the crackling.

"God, you're dumb!" Andries said. "You're going to get it! Dumb arse!"

I was too depressed to retort. Besides, I knew he was right. I was dumb. I should have run when he told me to.

"Come on," I said.

One of many small groups of children, each child carrying his little bag of crackling, we trod the long road home in the cold winter afternoon.

There was tension in the house that night. When I got back, Aunt Liza had listened to the story in silence. The beating or scolding I expected did not come. But Aunt Liza changed while she listened, became remote and withdrawn. When Uncle Sam came home she told him what had happened. He, too, just looked at me and became more remote and withdrawn than usual. They were waiting for something; their tension reached out to me, and I waited with them, anxious, apprehensive.

The thing we waited for came while we were having

our supper. We heard a carriage pull up outside.

"Here it is," Uncle Sam said, and got up.

Aunt Liza leaned back from the table and put her hands in her lap, fingers intertwined, a cold, unseeing look in her eyes.

Before Uncle Sam reached the door, it burst open. A tall, broad, white man strode in. Behind him came the three boys. The one I had attacked had swollen lips and a puffy left eye.

"Evening, *baas*," Uncle Sam murmured.

"That's him," the bigger boy said, pointing at me.

The white man stared till I lowered my eyes.

"Well?" he said.

"He's sorry, *baas*," Uncle Sam said quickly. "I've given him a hiding he won't forget soon. You know how it is, *baas*. He's new here, the child of a relative in Johannesburg, and they don't all know how to behave there. You know how it is in the big towns, *baas*." The plea in Uncle Sam's voice had grown more pronounced as he went on. He turned to me. "Tell the *baas* and young *basies* how sorry you are, Lee."

I looked at Aunt Liza and something in her lifelessness made me stubborn in spite of my fear.

"He insulted my father," I said.

The white man smiled.

"See, Sam, your hiding couldn't have been good."

There was a flicker of life in Aunt Liza's eyes. For a brief moment she saw me, looked at me, warmly,

59

lovingly; then her eyes went dead again.

"He's only a child, *baas*," Uncle Sam murmured.

"You stubborn too, Sam?"

"No, *baas*."

"Good. Then teach him, Sam. If you and he are to live here, you must teach him. Well—?"

"Yes, *baas*."

Uncle Sam went into the other room and returned with a thick leather thong. He wound it once round his hand and advanced on me. The man and the boys leaned against the door, watching. I looked at Aunt Liza's face. Though there was no sign of life or feeling on it, I knew suddenly, instinctively, that she wanted me not to cry.

Bitterly, Uncle Sam said: "You must never lift your hand to a white person. No matter what happens, you must never lift your hand to a white person. . . ."

He lifted the strap and brought it down on my back. I clenched my teeth and stared at Aunt Liza. I did not cry with the first three strokes. Then, suddenly, Aunt Liza went limp. Tears showed in her eyes. The thong came down on my back again and again. I screamed and begged for mercy. I grovelled at Uncle Sam's feet, begging him to stop, promising never to lift my hand to any white person. . . .

At last the white man's voice said: "All right, Sam."

Uncle Sam stopped. I lay whimpering on the floor. Aunt Liza sat like one in a trance.

"Is he still stubborn, Sam?"

"Tell the *baas* and *basies* you are sorry."

"I'm sorry," I said.

"Bet his father is one of those who believe in equality."

"His father is dead," Aunt Liza said.

"Good night, Sam."

"Good night, *baas*. Sorry about this."

"All right, Sam." He opened the door. The boys went out first, then he followed. "Good night, Liza."

Aunt Liza did not answer. The door shut behind the white folk, and soon we heard their trap moving away. Uncle Sam flung the thong viciously against the door, slumped down on the bench, folded his arms on the table, and buried his head on his arms. Aunt Liza moved away from him, sat down on the floor beside me, and lifted me into her large lap. She sat rocking my body. Uncle Sam began to sob softly. After some time he raised his head and looked at us.

"Explain to the child, Liza," he said.

"You explain," Aunt Liza said bitterly. "You are the man. You did the beating. You are the head of the family. This is a man's world. You do the explaining."

"Please, Liza."

"You should be happy. The whites are satisfied. We can go on now."

With me in her arms, Aunt Liza got up. She carried me into the other room. The food on the table re-

61

mained half-eaten. She laid me on the bed on my stomach, smeared fat on my back, then covered me with the blankets. She undressed and got into bed beside me. She cuddled me close, warmed me with her own body. With her big hand on my cheek, she rocked me, first to silence, then to sleep.

For the only time during my stay there, I slept on a bed in Elsburg.

When I woke next morning, Uncle Sam had gone. Aunt Liza only once referred to the beating he had given me. It was in the late afternoon, when I returned with the day's cow dung.

"It hurt him," she said. "You'll understand one day."

That night Uncle Sam brought me an orange, a bag of boiled sweets, and a dirty old picture book. He smiled as he gave them to me, rather anxiously. When I smiled back at him, he seemed to relax. He put his hand on my head, started to say something, then changed his mind and took his seat by the fire.

Aunt Liza looked up from the floor, where she dished out the food.

"It's all right, old man," she murmured.

"One day . . ." Uncle Sam said.

"It's all right," Aunt Liza repeated insistently.

Charity Waciuma

As more Africans go to school (and some travel overseas for education or business) Africa is rapidly becoming more and more "modern." The African past is ebbing away.

Our next author bridges the gap between two different ways of life by describing her relationship with her grandfather. Charity Waciuma belongs to the modern generation of Kenya, while her grandfather belongs to the traditional African society. All this she tells in her autobiography, *Daughter of Mumbi.*

Her own father, trained in Western medicine, worked at a local health center. Charity's book gives a vivid account of the clash between the traditional African medicine of her grandfather's world and her father's new medicine. She describes other clashes too, including the clash between the traditional religious beliefs of her grandfather and the Christian beliefs of the Western world which her own parents adopted.

But the greatest clash of all resulted from the white

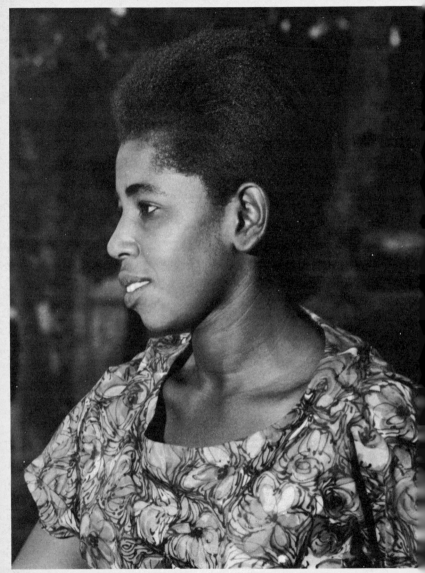

Charity Waciuma

settlers' theft of land belonging to the Africans in Kenya. The bitterness over land, as Charity shows in her book, finally overflowed in the Mau Mau protest movement.

The effort to get African lands back from the white settlers required education "in the white man's ways and his knowledge," as Charity says. This education was exactly what she and other young Kenyans acquired. And African parents were eager to send their children to school—at first mostly in mud huts, but now also in modern buildings of stone and concrete.

Charity enjoyed her grandfather's stories about the past. She longed for the time recalled in his stories to come again. But, as she says, she "knew with sadness that it never would."

Things have indeed changed in Africa. Charity Waciuma has changed too. She is married to a Biafran Veterinary Pathologist and with their four children they live in Zambia. Charity is a schoolteacher as well as a trained journalist and the author of three books—very different from the role of a young woman in her grandfather's day.

Grandfather and Granddaughter

As my grandfather grew older we would see him continually daydreaming of the time in his own youth when he was a warrior and fought the Masai.

In one raid he lost his brother but returned with a young woman called Nyokabi who became his second wife. Her great beauty still shone out even though she was so old. Nyokabi was calm and kind and gentle, but when she moved she went as swift as the wind. But my own grandmother, the first wife, had a tough temper and a quick tongue which often brought her a beating from my grandfather.

On our Sunday visits we grandchildren would fetch water for her from the river and she would cook for us a delicious calabash full of muthura, made from millet [grain], bananas and sweet potatoes. She also prepared njugu—small tasty peas.

It was fun to sit and listen to grandfather's stories, though he often reminded us that, when he was young, girls were not allowed to sit near when the elders were discussing such things. For this reason I was glad I was not alive in those days.

But in my heart of hearts, I wished I had known Mugo and Kinyanjui and the great giant who lived in the forest and had one big eye, one leg and two mouths—one for swallowing flies and the other for eating human beings. This giant had fire on his tail and carried a bell. It was said that anyone who saw the light of the fire or heard the sound of the bell would become rooted to the spot, powerless to move.

When the herdsman brought my grandfather's goats and cattle to the compound in the evening, this was the signal for us to start our four-mile journey home. My cousins used to come with us halfway and, before we parted, we would sit by the side of the road and play one or other of our traditional children's games.

One was called "fivestones"—throwing one stone into the air and quickly seizing another before the first came down again and was caught. Another was "ndama"—two rows of eight holes supposed to be cattle bomas (stockades), with stones to represent the cattle. The object was to move your stones to end up opposite a hole of another player and take all his "cattle."

Our road home led through a small forest and once we came face to face with what looked like a fox in the picture books. As we have been told that Kenya has no foxes, it was probably a jackal secretly glinting at us on the path. It did not frighten us, but we were scared of the general reputation of the place. People said there were mocking ghosts there, tall, white creatures who slapped and pulled the ears of evening travelers.

I suppose I only half believed these tales, but I still keep an eye for ghosts in the forests, and I do not travel through them at night.

Although my grandfather had a large shamba [farm] to divide among his sons, it was not enough for my father, who gave his share of the inheritance to be divided among his brothers. He bought land from a man of another clan who had no children. The members of that clan were not happy about this transfer. We had a lot of trouble about the boundaries and sometimes they stole our crops.

My father did not believe in witchcraft but this did not deter him from using it against thieves who did. He arranged to have a spell placed on anyone who had stolen his property.

The witch doctor's procedures were fascinating. He came with his bag of magic slung over his right shoulder. First he kindled a small fire on the shamba to warm himself. Sitting beside it he took a hen's leg from the bag and declared, as he broke it, "May the thieves' legs be smashed as is this hen's leg if they do not return the stolen maize [corn] crop."

He also licked a snakeskin and the tails of lizards and chameleons during the ceremony as part of the spell. Then as he damped down the fire he cursed again, saying, "As these flames die so may the thief. May his family wither as the twigs crumble to ashes in the fire."

Within seven days those who were guilty went to the witch doctor and confessed. On his instructions they returned the stolen maize by night so we never discovered who was responsible. We had occasion to use this magic more than once and it was always successful.

We lived in a house provided by the government, so my mother had a long walk of four miles to the shamba. On the way she would knit for us although she was also carrying food for our midday meal. It was very tiring for her carrying home the load of food, secured on her back in the traditional way by a strap across the top of her head. Our home was always spick and span and we children were well dressed and tidy. She never complained to my father about how hard she worked.

In Kihu, the month of bush-clearing, new areas of cultivation were prepared from the fallow. Four or five days of heavy rains were allowed to pass and then it was considered that the ground was moist enough for planting to begin. The women and girls went with pangas [machetes] and baskets of maize seeds. We planted maize in regular lines and scattered beans here and there among it. Sometimes as we worked, the rain poured down upon us.

At evening time during this season, most people would sit by the fires in their grass-thatched huts, telling stories and eating maize, cassava and potatoes which had been baked in the embers. I used to envy my girl friend, Wairimu, who I knew was sitting eating maize in her home while I was already in bed beneath a heavy blanket in mine.

We had to retire early after singing a few hymns and after we had severally said our prayers, kneeling beside the bed. My mother made us pray in turn. I asked God to help my mother, my father, our grannies and our dogs, which I thought were like little people, so quietly and piously did they sit while we prayed.

My mother used to employ women to help during

the weeding season. Sometimes they asked for payment in money and sometimes in maize or beans. They loved my mother because she worked alongside them. My job as a small girl, before I was old enough to go to school, was to look after the babies which the women brought and placed beside the field in which they were working.

When I look back, I remember how upset my grandfather was by our shapeless red and white striped Sunday School dresses. I wonder what he would say if he were alive today and could see his granddaughters driving cars, working as air hostesses and twisting the night away in jeans and slinky skirts.

R. Mugo Gatheru

Kenya, in East Africa, is today an independent nation. But before 1963 Kenya was a British colony for almost seventy years.

Kenya's agreeable climate and fertile land attracted British people to the colony. The colonial government encouraged British citizens to move to Kenya, even giving them money to settle and farm there. The government also gave the white settlers land which originally belonged to Kenya Africans. Severe frictions and hostilities developed. The main problem was land.

The white settlers received most of the fertile land, while the Africans were restricted to small, overcrowded areas. They were forbidden by law to farm the most profitable crops such as coffee. Yet they had to pay the very heavy taxes imposed by the colonial government. For most Kenya Africans, the only way to earn the money was to work on the farms of the white settlers at very low wages. The tax laws became a way to provide very cheap labor for the white settlers.

The Kenya Africans protested against the theft of their lands. One of the protest leaders was Jomo Kenyatta, who later became the first president of Kenya. But the colonial government passed laws to keep the Africans in check. One such law established the *Kipande* or "pass system" to keep Africans under strict control.

Kipande was later given up in Kenya, even before independence. But this "pass system" is still used in South Africa to control the Africans there, and to enforce *apartheid*.

One person whom Kipande affected personally as a youth

R. Mugo Gatheru

in Kenya was R. Mugo Gatheru. He describes the experience in the next selection taken from his autobiography, *Child of Two Worlds.*

Mugo was trained at the Medical Research Laboratory in Kenya. But he got into trouble on his first job because he wrote letters to newspapers protesting against racial discrimination and injustice. So Mugo took a new position as assistant editor of *The African Voice,* the newspaper of the Kenya African Union whose President was Jomo Kenyatta.

The young man wanted to go to the United States for further education. The British colonial regime in Kenya refused to give Mugo the "certificate of political good conduct" which the U.S. Consul in Kenya required before giving him a U.S. visa. This refusal was a result of the public letters he had written demanding justice and equality for all people—black and white.

Because he did not need a visa to travel to India, Mugo Gatheru went to India in 1949. From there he came to the United States, where he received an M.A. degree from New York University. He later studied law in London and Professor Gatheru is now teaching history and government at Sacramento State College, California.

I am Hit by a Night Stick

The Kenya Africans were sick and tired of insulting, humiliating, and discriminatory passes and the laws which had instituted these passes. The most hated pass of them all was called the Kipande which was like a registration certificate and which the Africans had to carry on their person at all times. An American friend of mine who saw this pass remarked to me that it was based on the assumption that a large number or proportion of the Africans were inherently dishonest.

The Kipande system was officially introduced in Kenya in 1921. Every male African above sixteen years of age had to be registered, fingerprinted, and issued with a registration certificate—Kipande. Kipande was different from the passport, the birth certificate, the identity cards in Britain, or social security numbers in the United States of America.

In Kenya a policeman could stop an African on the road or in the street and demand that he produce his Kipande—regardless of whether the African concerned was as wise as Socrates, as holy as St. Francis, or as piratical as Sir Francis Drake.

Kipande was also used to prevent the African laborer escaping distasteful employment or from unjust employers who had power to have him arrested and then fined, imprisoned, or both.

When Kenyatta took over the leadership of the Kenya African Union he announced publicly that the Africans had carried "Vipande" (plural for Kipande) long enough and that they should burn them if the Kenya Government refused to repeal the ordinance which had instituted the system. The alternative,

Kenyatta explained, was for the Kenya Government to issue Vipande to all the races of Kenya—the Europeans, the Asians, and the Africans.

The Africans, at that time, were seriously prepared to take action, illegal if necessary, to abolish Vipande whether the Government liked it or not. Mass meetings were held all over Kenya at which a lot of money was collected to buy wood for a big fire at the centre of Nairobi city on which all the Africans would burn their Vipande. This was to be an historic fire!

Quickly and wisely the Kenya Government promised the African leaders that the Kipande system would be repealed forthwith and that a system of identity cards for all the races in Kenya would replace it.

The Africans welcomed the government promise and in 1950 the Kipande system was abolished. But the scars of Kipande remained. In the thirty years of its existence Kipande caused great humiliation and hardship and was a constant grievance among my people. It cannot be said that the British Government knew nothing of this: when sending Kenyatta to England on various occasions from 1929 onwards the Africans instructed him to speak not only about the thorny problems of land but also to protest about Kipande.

A well-known missionary, and one of the few well-wishers of the Kenya Africans among the Europeans there, complained in a letter to the London *Times* of June 1938 that not less than 50,000 Africans in Kenya had been jailed since 1920 for failure to produce Vipande—an average of 5000 Africans per year!

When the Kenya Government announced officially in 1948 that the Kipande system would be abolished, the Kenya settlers, as was expected, resisted strongly. The instrument which they had used so long in keeping the African laborers in a state of serfdom was now being lifted. They accused the Government of yielding to "African agitators" and "irresponsible demagogues!" The settlers did not stop to ask themselves what would be the effect of the frustrated anger of the Kenya Africans. They did not understand that no human being, of whatever nationality, can keep on indefinitely without breaking through such frustration. After all, the Kenya Africans had carried their Vipande on their persons from 1921 to 1950, and yet the Kipande was only one of innumerable grievances.

The Europeans and the Asians were free from having Vipande. The psychological effect of the Kipande system was equal to that of an African calling a European "Bwana" instead of "Mr." or of a European calling a seventy-year-old African "boy," or referring to the "natives" without a capital "N," or "native locations" in the city instead of "African sections."

The Africans were constantly worried by these passes. I remember full well that, whenever my father mislaid his Kipande, he was as much worried and unhappy as if he had been an important government official accused of accepting a vicuna coat from a private citizen!

There were also numerous other passes which were equally insulting and principally the so-called "Red-Book" issued by the Labor Exchange, which every African domestic servant was required to carry. In the Red-Book the character of the African concerned, the amount of pay he was receiving, and the cause of dismissal were to be recorded.

I remember well one afternoon when I was walking with Muchaba, who had been my chief aide during my *irua* or circumcision ceremony. We were in Pangani, one of the sections of Nairobi, when we heard a voice far away call "Simama" or "Halt!"

We did not pay too much attention since we were discussing family matters. Suddenly, we heard another voice shouting loudly: "You! Stop there!"

We looked back and saw two policemen hurrying towards us. We suddenly had butterflies in our stomachs. We stopped and waited for them and, as they were approaching us, I whispered to Muchaba:

"Do you have your Kipande with you?"

"No, I don't have it," he replied.

"I don't have mine either."

"We'll catch hell now," Muchaba said.

The two policemen came up to us.

"Why didn't you stop at once when we called you?" the first one asked. And the second one, sarcastically:

"Who do you think you are?" even before we had a chance to reply.

"At first we didn't know you were calling to us, sirs," Muchaba said. "We are very sorry."

"No, you look like lawbreakers, like most of the Kikuyu," one policeman said.

"Show us your Kipande quickly!" the second one demanded.

"I don't have mine. I have just forgotten it," Muchaba replied.

"Where?"

"Where I work," Muchaba said.

"Where and for whom do you work?" asked the policeman.

"I work for a European lady just near the Fair View Hotel."

"What do you do?"

"I am a cook," Muchaba replied.

"Do you have any other pass as an identification?" asked the policeman.

"No. But I can give you my employer's address and the telephone number if you like," Muchaba said.

"Idiot!" shouted the policeman. "How stupid can you get? Do you expect us to make telephone calls for all criminals we arrest without their Vipande? We are not your telephone operators."

"What can I do then?" asked Muchaba.

"Carry your Kipande with you," replied the police-man. "Incidentally, who is this fellow here with his arms folded like a great bwana. Do you have your Kipande?" They turned to me.

"No, I don't have it. I have never had a formal Kipande," I said.

"What!" they both exclaimed thunderously.

"When I joined the Medical Department in 1945, the Senior Medical Officer sent me to the Labor Exchange to obtain my Kipande but I found out that the copies of the formal Kipande were exhausted. I was given an emergency certificate and told to get a formal Kipande later on," I explained.

"Are you still in the Medical Department?" they asked.

"No, I am working for the Kenya African Union as an assistant editor," I said.

"Where do you live?" they asked.

"Kaloleni," I replied.

"Just because you are working for that trouble-making KAU you think you don't have to carry Kipande?"

"No, that is not the reason. I just forgot my emergency certificate. I don't think that KAU is trouble making. We fight for the rights of everyone in Kenya, including the police," I said.

They looked at each other, confused.

79

"Do you have any other papers as identification?" they asked.

"I have some papers with the letterheading of the Kenya African Union."

"We are not interested in letterheads. We want official documents. Any fool can produce letterheads."

This comedy finally ended and they decided to take us to the police station.

We walked in front of them and they followed us. As we were walking I tried to get a handkerchief from my pocket to blow my nose. One policeman thought that I was insulting him by putting my hands in my pocket like a big bwana and hit me on my shoulder with his night stick. He hit me hard. I tried to explain to him that my nose was running but I saw he was ready to hit me again, and so I kept quiet. Muchaba said nothing.

As we approached the police station I heard somebody calling:

"Hey you, that's Mr. Mathu's man. What did he do?"

Muchaba and I were afraid to look back in case we should be hit again. The two policemen answered the call and then suddenly told us to stop. We turned round and saw two other policemen coming towards us. I recognized one of them. He was my classmate at Kambui Primary School and he knew both Muchaba and me full well. We were relieved and happy!

The four policemen conferred together, and the

one who knew us explained to his colleagues that we must have been telling the truth, and that we should not be arrested. Two of them agreed but the third still wanted to go to the police station.

At last they let us go, but by then Muchaba was very late in returning to his work. His employer was very, very angry, as her dinner was late. Muchaba had not telephoned and she had no idea where to find him.

I advised Muchaba to take a taxi but there was none in sight. It was getting too late. Finally he took a bus and, when he arrived at his employer's home, he found her waiting near the gate holding a pen.

"Bring your Red-Book right away. You have no job now. You are entirely unreliable, a lazy, untrustworthy African. I hate you bloody niggers," she said.

Muchaba had no chance to explain anything. He was told to pack up his belongings and leave at once. He had some heavy luggage and couldn't move it all at once and so he took it bit by bit to the nearest street. Finally he took a taxi and came to my place. I took a chance and let him stay with me for the night! If the police had woken me up in the night and found him with me, both of us would have been in trouble.

That evening, as he had never learnt to read or write English, Muchaba asked me to tell him what had been written in his Red-Book. I knew Muchaba very well to be a sensitive and intelligent man and was sickened to read: "He is quick in his work; he likes sweet things and may steal sugar if he has a chance; sometimes his thinking is like that of an eleven-year-old child." When Muchaba heard this he was so angry that he burnt the book. I cannot blame him for this.

But it put him in serious difficulty as no one would give him another job unless he produced the book, even this one with its permanent defamatory record. It was more than a month before the Labor Exchange agreed to issue Muchaba with a new book (I can only liken the process to that when one loses a passport), and then he was able to get another job working as a cook for a wealthy Indian businessman.

Muchaba's story can also illustrate the considerable licence allowed by their superiors to the ordinary police force, at that time largely illiterate, which in itself contributed to the atmosphere of European superiority and power which sapped the resistance of the unorganized African population.

In the evenings the police could knock on the door of any African in the African locations and demand to know how many people were sleeping there, how many had Kipande, and proof of where they were working. This could have happened to any African rooming place, and almost always the police called about eleven o'clock or midnight.

In some cases, a man and his wife might be sleeping peacefully but they had to open the door quickly.

Police would then ask the man to produce Kipande and to say where he was working. They would search everywhere with their flashlights and, if they were satisfied, would leave the place without even saying sorry to the couple they had awakened.

I remember full well when the police knocked up one of my uncles at about 12.45 A.M. When three policemen entered the room my uncle and his wife were trying to fix their pajamas. One of the policemen shouted:

"How many people do you have in this room, eh?"

"Only my wife and myself, sir."

"How many people do you usually accommodate?" the second policeman demanded.

"None at all except my wife."

"My wife, my wife," the third policeman shouted. "How do we know she isn't just a prostitute from Manjengo, eh?"

"No! No! You have it all wrong. This is my own legal wife and if you insist on disagreeing with me please take me to the police station," Uncle protested vehemently. His pride and dignity were badly shaken. Utterly hurt.

The three policemen left. They had caused great upset and inconvenience to my uncle and his wife but he had no remedy. He could not sue the Police Department which could always say, "They did this in the course of their duty to uproot undesirable natives"—an excuse invariably accepted by their superiors.

I would illustrate the general attitude of their superiors to the police by quoting from *The Report on the Committee on Police Terms of Service* (1942), which among other things says:

> The evidence submitted to us indicates that, in general, the illiterate African makes a better policeman than a literate African. The latter is less amenable to discipline and is reluctant to undertake the menial tasks which sometimes fall to the lot of ordinary constables. That being so, it seems to us that the policy of recruiting literates should be pursued with great caution, and that no special inducements by way of salary are necessary. In fact, we venture to go so far as to recommend the abolition of literacy allowance for new entrants.

In the rural area it was difficult for me to realize that the Africans were always accorded the worst treatment. The city life taught me this.

Babs Fafunwa

Many Africans would like to visit the United States. They look forward to being welcomed by the Statue of Liberty to the land of plenty, the land of freedom and equality.

By the time an African leaves the U.S. he has seen two equally astonishing Americas—one beautiful, the other ugly. He is impressed by the free schools for everyone and the widespread medical care. There are also the splendid highways and the electrical gadgets that make life easier. The African is impressed by the American drive to achieve. He meets some warm-hearted people and makes a few close friends.

But the African sees America not only as the land of liberty but also as the land of freedom and justice denied. He experiences discrimination even in some Christian

Babs Fafunwa

churches—of all places! He is perplexed that the U.S. Congress had to pass a Civil Rights Act to guarantee equality—in the land of equality!

Now he is convinced that, East or West, home is the best. Most Africans abroad agree with what one African said about his longing to return to his homeland: "Africa, my Africa, is the best."

One African visitor was Babs Fafunwa who came to Florida in 1948 to study at Bethune-Cookman College. After earning his doctoral degree from New York University, Dr. Fafunwa returned home to Nigeria in 1956. (The nation achieved independence from the British four years later.) He worked for a time as a public-relations manager for Esso Oil. Later he became Head of the College of Education at the University of Nigeria. Since 1967 Professor Fafunwa has been the Dean of the Faculty of Education, University of Ife, also in Nigeria.

In the following selection, written for the *Chicago Defender* while he was a student in this country, Dr. Fafunwa describes some of his experiences in the United States of America.

An African's Adventures in America

Since my arrival in this country to study, I have met over fifty African students during my vacations. In exchanging views with them I found that most of our impressions after arriving on the American soil are almost identical. Everything about him is new, the student finds out.

He is mobbed by a group of inquiring reporters who ask: What is your name? Where do you come from? What is your impression about America? How many wives has your father? Are you married? Is it true that you buy women in Africa? Are you a prince? Is your father a king or a gold miner?

The shooting of flash bulbs adds to the confusion. This barrage is an indication of what the student is to experience as he moves from one part of the United States to another.

One of my most exciting experiences happened when I arrived in New York City. On that day it had one of its greatest snowfalls, and what's more I had never seen snow in my life. That day, my heavy overcoat was no solution to my dilemma. As I stepped out of the airplane I was baptized with the unusually biting cold. I was shaken to the bones and all my limbs were trembling. The woman in me subdued the man and my eyes were shedding tears like an Arabian gum tree. That night I slept in my overcoat, suit and all. The temperature was 19° F. and the lowest temperature I have ever seen in Nigeria is 60°.

Till I landed in New York I had never met an American Negro. My impression was that since the Negro has been living there for the past three hundred years or more he ought to have intermarried with the whites so that his color should be at least lighter than my own. (By the way, I am ebony black and I'd like to be twice as dark.) But when I landed I saw a Negro darker than myself. I thought he was an African who came a little earlier than I did. I rushed to him with all the happiness and the joy of finding a kinsman in this great metropolis. I said, "Hello, dear, when did you come?" He looked at me with cold surprise. I later found that he must have been here three hundred years, for his speech is as entirely strange to me as mine to him.

The student who hails from the British sphere of influence in Africa finds on getting here that America's ideas of democracy are in conflict, in a way, to those of Britain. The average Englishman admits that a Lord Jim is his "better." He does not resent his betters nor put himself on an equal basis with them nor does he wish to do so. The American, on the other hand, rejects all ideas of class. Everybody is "Hey" or "Say, Mister."

The student finds that democracy works fairly well in the North and otherwise in the South. He finds in the North that competition is tough, but in the South segregation and discrimination stare him in the face. I remember one day when the African students at Bethune-Cookman College in Florida were on their way back to school after giving an African program at a church. We stopped at a filling station for some refreshments.

A policeman entered and said, "Where are you 'niggers' from?"

We quickly responded that we were not niggers but African students.

"I say you are niggers," he shouted.

"No, 'officer of peace,' we are not."

"I say you are niggers," he affirmed, and to make it more positive he rested his hand on his gun. Like cowards we had to admit that we were niggers—at least by keeping silent!

We have been turned out of restaurants in the South several times despite our appeal to the people in charge that we are strangers and that such action is un-American since it is bad public relations for America, the arena of democracy. It is very encouraging, however, to find that once in a while we meet people in the South who give us very good breaks, help and assistance. Once a white fellow gave me a ride, and as I entered I sat at the back, for you are not supposed to sit with a white. He said, "Come to the front—I am no chauffeur." I was amused indeed.

The denial of the ballot box to Negroes in some parts of the South makes the average African student become a little disillusioned about American democracy. He believed before coming to America that this country is an arsenal of democracy, but to his dismay he finds that America is just learning like Africa to be democratic. Who knows, the whole world might soon copy Africa as regards true democracy.

The student finds that the United States, unlike

Africa, is a "woman's paradise." He becomes oriented to what is called "a woman's privilege." He discovers that fifty per cent or more of all the property in the United States is owned by women. In America when a man dies, he leaves all his wealth to his widow, for the son is expected to make his own way in the world. In case the property is divided among the children, the daughters have shares equal to—if not more than— the sons'. The student also finds that the parents are more inclined to educate the girl than the boy. All of these are just the opposite of the African custom.

This is not all. He finds that there are more divorce cases in America, where people marry but one. In Africa men have the privilege of marrying two or more wives, all depending on the husband's economic back-stay. He finds also that American women are more jealous than their African counterparts when it comes to love affairs.

Once a friend said, "Babs, I learn that you buy wives in Africa."

I replied, "Yes, we do and that is why they are dearer to us than yours to you."

But the truth is that the dowry a husband pays is a gift given to the parents as equipment fee for the bride. This amount is used to buy all the necessities a bride needs before her marriage. This particular aspect of our social life has been willfully misrep-resented and we hope our American friends will understand. We love our women as passionately as the Americans and we are not in the habit of ill-treating them or regarding them as chattels.

The first thing an African student is told is that he should get Americanized, socialize with the girls, forgo the English wide trousers for the American narrow pants, his little coat for the long heavy coat. He finds that table manners in America vary considerably from what he had been used to at home. He used fork, knife, spoon, etc., while the Americans use the fork for everything on the table except soup.

He therefore has to unlearn what he had learned previously and get adjusted to the American way of life. But the pity is that he has to unlearn what he is learning now in order to fit into his own pattern on his return home: British way to American way back to British way again, while at the same time he has to take care of his culture the African way.

Legson Kayira

A poverty-stricken African boy woke up one morning with a dream and a determination—to go to America for a college education.

How would he get there? Walk. Yes, walk from his village in Nyasaland to Port Said in Egypt. The distance is about 4000 miles. From Port Said he hoped to work his passage on a cargo ship bound for the United States.

Legson Didimu Kayira was born into a very poor home in the village of Mpale. It was only with great difficulty that his family could pay his school fees of less than 50 cents a year. But by the time he was nine or ten years old Didimu had learned the value of education. Every day he walked eight miles each way to attend school. Shortly after his father died, Didimu entered a high school, Livingstonia, about two hundred miles away from his home.

Legson Kayira

In Nyasaland most Africans fortunate enough to attend high school returned home to teach young children in local schools. There was no university in the country. But Didimu was determined to get more education—in America.

His mother was surprised and shocked to learn that Didimu wanted to go away to America. America? Where is that? How far is it? How will you get there? How long will it take?

To reassure his mother Didimu replied, "Five days." Five days to walk from Nyasaland to America!

His mother believed him. She said goodbye in their traditional manner. And off went Kayira with two books, two shirts, one pair of shorts, a blanket, a map, and a few cents on a journey his mother believed would be a five-day walk to America. He was about eighteen years old.

Five days! It took him two years to walk the nearly 2500 miles from his village to Khartoum, capital city of the Sudan. On the way he sometimes walked along roads, at other times on tracks through the forest. He encountered bruises and sicknesses, joys and tears. He met many kind people in rural villages, and a few hostile ones. Many times he could not speak the same language as the people he met. Sometimes he stayed in one place long enough to earn some money. All these adventures add to the warmth of his moving autobiography, *I Will Try*.

Events took a turn for the better in Khartoum because of the humanity of one man and the goodness of some people here in the United States. Didimu had applied by mail to Skagit Valley College in the state of Washington. The people of the college town raised enough money to pay for his transportation by air. These Americans all wanted to help this young African's dream come true.

In 1964, after four years at Skagit Valley College and the University of Washington, Legson Didimu Kayira returned home to his village. Independence was in the air. Nyasaland was about to emerge from colonial status under the British as the independent nation of Malawi. In the following selection from *I Will Try* Legson Kayira tells of his homecoming and the birth of the new nation of Malawi.

Homecoming

Isn't it a beautiful coincidence that I should be writing this portion of the book under the roof of my mother's house? Oh no, I am not dreaming. I am really here.

I look to the east and I see a hill, a big one. I look to the west and I see another hill. Neither looks any taller or shorter than when I left it almost six years ago. There was a time when I scaled their heights and never dreamed I would not see them for as long as six years. These hills were part of my life and wherever I went, I would point to them and say, "There is my home."

My mother is still here. I know it because I have been reunited with her. In fact, I am looking at her now as I write this. She is still young-looking and still unable to comprehend the fact that America is considerably more than five days away on foot but only about a day by jet.

I surprised her. She did not know I was coming on that particular day. I had written to say that I expected to come home for the summer, but I never gave her the exact day. I realized that she would have been very excited had I been able to tell her the exact day of my arrival. (Excitement was part and parcel of my entire homecoming.) But I also realized that if I told her, she would spend the whole day waiting anxiously for her prodigal. If for some unforeseen reason I failed to show up on that particular day, even if it were possible that I should show up the very next day, I feared I would find her in a miserable mood.

I flew to Blantyre [in southern Malawi] from Seattle in the company of Mr. Lane Smith, a reporter for the Seattle *Times*, who, among other things, was to cover Nyasaland's Independence celebrations. We traveled by Land Rover from Blantyre to Mpale, my village, arriving here a little before noon on a sunny Saturday. My mother and my sister were sitting in front of the house. They have changed houses since I left, and if it were not for the help of an old friend who hitchhiked a ride with us, Mr. Smith and I would have been temporarily lost.

The Land Rover pulled in a few yards from where they were sitting. I daresay they were startled, because few cars, if any, had ever stopped here.

I jumped out, and no sooner had I done so than my mother recognized me. Quick as a wink the neighbors learned I had come. Already Mr. Smith was getting the credit for bringing me home!

My brother and my sister are both here. They are pupils at one of the schools I attended myself. They were not able to recognize me any more than I could recognize them. They have grown up. My brother seems very quiet, very reserved. He stammers when he speaks, and he tells me he began stammering less than two years ago.

I have been here in my old home for several days now and I am now convinced that I am not dreaming. I have met again a good many of the people who lived here when I also lived here. Some of them, of course, have left us for the next world. Some are already stooping down when they walk by reason of the heavy weight of age. Those who were born after I left do not know me and they still run away from me.

Most of the people say that I have changed, that I do not look as I did before. I say they have changed too, that the whole village has changed. Could it be that we all have changed? Yet I would have recognized my mother anywhere, and she was able to recognize me in no time at all.

However, my village looks very different, and for a time I was almost convinced that nobody understood me, although I spoke in my own language—theirs too, by the way.

Now that I am sitting here, almost fully reunited

with my beginnings, I look back to that October morning almost six years ago. "You are mad, you are really mad," my cousin Kaliyokha had said. He is still here and he still thinks I am mad. I may have had a wild dream then, but even with that wild dream I could hardly have believed I would get where I was going and that one day I would fly back home for a holiday. I remember my mother spitting in my face, giving me her short but classic advice.

"God is powerful," one woman cried when she came to embrace me that Saturday morning I arrived in Mpale. "He has brought our child home!"

God is powerful, that we know. I am wondering, though, what would have become of me if I had not left or if I had abandoned my plans on the way and given up. Well, I do not know because I did not give up. Possibly I would be working somewhere in the country and raising a family.

During the short period since I have been home I have visited most of my relatives and old friends, even those who live a considerable distance from my village. I have been to see the family of our ex-family doctor. I am told that the doctor himself was not able to survive the bite of a black mamba.

I have already visited my old school, Livingstonia. It has changed too to some extent but it still gives one the feeling and the urge for scholarship. The man who built it must have had monumental plans for it. I have

99

already seen several new primary schools. In all these schools I have seen the happy pupils, whose faces beam at one with smiles of appreciation of their opportunities, and encouragement of their time. They may not have the same opportunities as their American counterparts, but they are accepting all that their country can possibly give them.

These pupils seem to take their work seriously. It is a matter of competition, especially for those who have their hearts set on some college or university. They *must* get there. For them this is no longer a world of complacency as it may have been for their fathers. They know that the future of their country lies in their hands.

In the old days one went to school to learn how to read and write and one survived pretty well. These young people realize now that for them and their country to survive, they will need more than just learning how to read and write. Their philosophy is not: "Ask and you shall receive." Rather it is: "Labor and you shall gain."

How difficult is it to get an American scholarship? This is the question I have been asked many times by these young people. I do not know what the answer is. I cannot answer for any country. I cannot answer for any university, even for my own University of Washington. I do not know, but like my questioners I would wish it were easier.

Is it possible for one from here to enter a secondary school in America? This is another question that they have often asked me. I should think so. I know of some high schools that have exchange programs with other countries. I should think this is one of the most constructive ways of cultivating friendship between or among nations.

In some cases this exchange should prove better than if it were done on a college level. Why do I think so? Well, I believe that misunderstanding often breeds conflict, and that if countries encouraged the exchange of their young people to study in other countries, even for a short time and at a time when they have not yet acquired lifelong traditional ideas, often wrong ideas, of other cultures, maybe something could be done toward clearing this cloud of misunderstanding that prevails over us all.

It looks as if I have just waked up from a long sleep with a long dream that took me to far distant lands, to the very edge of the earth. I am thinking of my homes in Mount Vernon [in Washington state] and in Seattle, as well as my original home here where I am now. Indeed, I can say that I feel like a child of two nations, appreciating two cultures, one that I was born to and the other that was once foreign to me, but which is now becoming familiar. I know that I have almost failed to make a perfect adjustment in the former culture, but I also know that this is an error not to be repeated again.

Most people, including my mother, are surprised to learn that I have not come back here for good, that I shall be here for three months only.

"What is it that you are looking for?" they ask me.

"See so-and-so," my mother says. "He is younger than you are, but he is already working."

"You must marry now," the big men of the village tell me. "Settle down."

There is nothing I am looking for, I try to tell them. Staying at home now would not make any more sense than if I had stayed home six years ago. Surely I have been to America, and although this alone would give me a different outlook, my purpose for going there was to obtain an education. I have not yet graduated from my university. I have to comfort my mother by assuring her that this goal will be attained before the end of a year. After that, there will be a year or two of postgraduate work. At any rate, I should be back here within three years.

The soldiers who had been parading came to a stop and stood at attention. They were in the grounds of the huge Central Stadium of Blantyre-Limbe.

Thousands of spectators moved on their seats and exchanged whispers with their neighbors, then there was silence again. Only the sound of the clock could be heard, slowly ticking toward midnight and at the same time building up impatience and anxiety in the souls of the spectators.

"God bless our gracious Queen . . ." The serious band played the noble anthem. Thousands were standing. Then there was a short period of darkness as the lights in the stadium were turned off, then light again. The proud Union Jack had finally come down and the world's newest flag, bearing the colors of black, red, and green, had unfurled and was now flying. Then the world's newest anthem, "O God Bless Our Land of Malawi," was played:

> O God bless our land of Malawi,
> Keep it a land of peace,
> Put down each and every enemy,
> Hunger, disease, envy.
> Join together all our hearts as one,
> That we be free from fear.
> Bless our leader, each and everyone,
> And Mother Malawi.

There was an outburst of cheers and singing. A new nation had been born and they called it Malawi.

How touching it is to witness one's country's triumph of becoming free. How beautiful it is! It gives one a feeling of pride and of achievement. It makes one proud, as one's parents are proud of their baby, and proud of one's time and generation.

103

Future generations of Malawi will inherit independence and freedom. They will not have the same feelings for it as the Malawians of this day. They will probably take it for granted. Those today who have worked hard for it know that it is only by hard work that this independence will survive.

One may look at the past, the near past, in the history of Nyasaland, now Malawi. It has not been much longer than seventy-three years that the Union Jack has flown over this land, and during this time the people have struggled and advanced to independence. Now the land is free and so are its people.

We know that with the spirit that has directed this country and its people in the past, the independence of this country can be assured. My people know how they fought for freedom, how many people lost their lives so others could be free. They know that if we should lose this independence, the next struggle for it could be more difficult, more ruthless, and might be useless.

On July 6, 1964, I wrote for the Seattle *Times:*

"Nine score and eight years ago, a few men later to be the prideful forefathers of one of the greatest nations ever to be created by the Lord, took one of the boldest steps in the history of mankind: They decided to declare themselves free and independent of the mighty Empire of Britain.

"They were few, but very dedicated. They were

alone, but trusting in the great powers of their Maker.

"They may have been ridiculed and laughed at; they may have doubted their own decision, but they held on to it fast and strong, and what was then a desire of the few came, in their future generations, to be a desire of the millions.

"Nine score and eight years later, a new nation has been born, created and founded by one Dr. H. Kamuzu Banda and freed, as it were, from the same grand Empire.

"Were the Lord to instruct that the Americans of that day should return to America today, how proud would they be to find that the little nation they founded is now far beyond what their petty imaginations could then conceive!

"Now, it is Malawi that takes the same bold step. She has decided to declare herself free and independent.

"There may be some who are laughing at Malawi now; there may be some who are waiting to see what will happen to her, but she is holding on to her decision.

"In the streets, on the trails, in the towns, in the villages, hundreds upon hundreds of Malawians sing and cheer and talk of the Grand Day. . . .

"This is their nation. They have helped found it, and if the Lord were to instruct that they should return to their nation, nine score and eight years from now, how proud they would be on that day to find that the nation they founded was still striving and surviving all odds!"

A salute to you, Malawi, and Godspeed. We have just begun to try.

Bibliography

The books from which the selections in this anthology were taken are available in the following editions.

A Royal African (formerly entitled *I Was a Savage*) by Prince Modupe. Frederick A. Praeger, Publishers.

Equiano's Travels: *The Interesting Narrative of the Life of Olaudah Equiano or Gustavus Vassa the African.* Abridged and edited by Paul Edwards. Frederick A. Praeger, Publishers.

The Narrow Path: *An African Childhood* by Francis Selormey. Frederick A. Praeger, Publishers.

Tell Freedom: *Memories of Africa* by Peter Abrahams.
Hardcover: Alfred A. Knopf, Inc.
Paperback: Collier Books (African/American Library), The Macmillan Company.

Daughter of Mumbi by Charity Waciuma.
Paperback: East African Publishing House, P.O. Box 30571, Nairobi, Kenya.

Child of Two Worlds: *A Kikuyu's Story* by R. Mugo Gatheru.
Hardcover: Frederick A. Praeger, Publishers.
Paperback: Humanities Press, Inc.
Anchor Books, Doubleday & Company, Inc.

I Will Try by Legson Kayira.
Hardcover: Doubleday & Company, Inc.
Paperback: Bantam Pathfinder, Bantam Books, Inc.

The article by Babs Fafunwa appears in **An African Treasury**, selected by Langston Hughes. Paperback: Pyramid Book, Pyramid Publications, Inc.

107

COMPILER'S NOTE: I wish to acknowledge the thoughtfulness of people whose assistance in several ways has made this book possible. I have a deep sense of gratitude to Mr. William Gray and Mr. James Gray, who made available to me their very rich collection of African books in the More Bookstore in San Francisco. And I was privileged to work with an exceptionally fine editor, Miss Janet Finnie of Random House, New York. My thanks also go to Mrs. Toni Morrison, herself a brilliant author, also of Random House, New York. Above all, my profound appreciation goes to my family and in particular my wife, Oluwaremilekun, whose love, patience, understanding, and critical reading of my manuscripts have always been most beneficial.

The photographs in this book are courtesy of the individual contributors except as follows. **Olaudah Equiano:** New York Public Library, Rare Book Room. **Peter Abrahams:** Alfred A. Knopf, Inc., New York. **Charity Waciuma:** East African Publishing House, Nairobi, Kenya. **Legson Kayira:** Seattle *Times* from Doubleday and Company, New York. **Endpaper:** Marc and Evelyne Bernheim (Rapho Guillumette).